Original title:
Xanthic Slivers Around the Elf Hoop

Copyright © 2025 Swan Charm
All rights reserved.

Author: Paula Raudsepp
ISBN HARDBACK: 978-1-80562-330-4
ISBN PAPERBACK: 978-1-80563-851-3

Golden Patrons of the Sylvan Court

In the heart of the whispering wood,
Golden patrons in glimmering hood,
Dancing lights in the twilight fade,
Guardians of secrets in shadows laid.

With laughter twinkling among the leaves,
They weave their magic as twilight weaves,
In circles of starlight, they spin their tales,
Through moonlit paths where adventure sails.

Crimson roses and silver dew,
Their gentle hands hold the night's soft hue,
Fables and dreams float on the breeze,
Sung by the winds with an ease to please.

Beneath the boughs where the old trees sigh,
They gather round, with a knowing eye,
Each secret kept, each wish set free,
In the courts of sylvan harmony.

So if you wander where shadows play,
And hear the laughter where fairies sway,
Remember the golden patrons' flight,
For they guard the magic of the night.

Luminous Paths of the Sylvan Herald

Through verdant woods where shadows play,
A narrow path winds soft and gay.
With torches bright, the fireflies dance,
Guiding the lost toward fate's sweet chance.

The sylvan herald lifts his gaze,
To stars that weave the night with praise.
In rustling leaves, secrets unfold,
Stories of dreams both brave and bold.

Beneath the boughs, the whispers flow,
Of ancient tales and forgotten woe.
Upon the moss, where spirits tread,
Hope springs eternal from dreams long dead.

Each step resounds with echoes near,
A melody that calms all fear.
With every turn, a new light forms,
Illuminating paths, defying storms.

Follow the map of stars aglow,
Where light and shadow intertwine slow.
For in this realm, where wonders start,
The sylvan herald guides each heart.

Golden Sparks Upon the Elfin Glade

In the glade where sunlight meet,
Golden sparks in joy do greet.
A land where laughter fills the air,
Every sprite and fae lays bare.

With gossamer wings that shimmer bright,
Elves of grace dance in delight.
Their steps a rhythm, soft and sweet,
An echo of the heart's own beat.

The flowers sway, a tender song,
In harmony where all belong.
The brook chuckles, a gentle tease,
As breezes whisper through the trees.

Each moment glows with magic rare,
Suspended in the golden air.
A tapestry where dreams entwine,
Golden sparks, in heart, divine.

So linger long upon this land,
Let hope and dreams in youth expand.
In the elfin glade, let spirits soar,
As golden sparks forever bore.

Celestial Whispers Under the Ancient Oaks

Beneath the boughs, where shadows play,
The ancient oaks hold wisdom's sway.
With every rustle, secrets glide,
A soothing murmur, nature's pride.

Celestial whispers ride the breeze,
Carried softly through the trees.
They speak of stars and worlds unseen,
Echoing dreams where hearts convene.

The roots entwined in earth rich and deep,
Guard tales of ages in their keep.
With every ring, a story told,
Of life in cycles, young and old.

In twilight's embrace, the magic spins,
As light cascades where darkness thins.
For in this realm, the night takes flight,
And dawn ignites the canvas bright.

So pause a moment, close your eyes,
Listen closely, hear the skies.
For under oaks, the cosmos stars,
Awake the dreams that have no bars.

Shining Reflections in the Enchanted Circle

In the circle where magic weaves,
Shining reflections dance like leaves.
Collecting dreams from every year,
In this sacred space, so dear.

Crystal lights weave stories old,
Tales of warmth against the cold.
Each shimmer speaks, a voice of grace,
As time unfolds in this hidden place.

The moon casts shadows, soft and long,
A soothing lullaby, nature's song.
In the heart of night, all fears dissolve,
Mysteries of fate around us revolve.

Beneath the stars, where wishes dwell,
From whispered wishes, magic swells.
The circle holds what hearts require,
Awakening hope, igniting fire.

So gather close and feel the light,
In the enchanted circle, bold and bright.
For in this realm, where wishes take flight,
Shining reflections guide us right.

Golden Gleams in Enchanted Rings

In the forest where magic blooms,
Golden glimmers break through the glooms.
Whispers of elves in harmony play,
As dawn's soft light claims the day.

Dancing shadows in the trees,
Catch the sun with graceful ease.
Every leaf a story spun,
In the glow of morning's run.

Rings of light on dewdrops rest,
Nature's jewels, simply blessed.
With every step, the secrets twine,
Binding hearts in the sacred vine.

Through meadows dressed in morning's gold,
Ancient tales of love unfold.
Magic lingers in the air,
A tapestry beyond compare.

So let the wanderers find their way,
Chasing dreams where sunbeams play.
In this realm of endless spring,
Hope and joy in golden rings.

Luminous Threads of the Woodland Dance

Underneath the twilight haze,
Luminous threads weave through the bays.
Echoes of laughter fill the night,
Fairy lights twinkling in flight.

Branches sway to the gentle tune,
Dancing softly beneath the moon.
With every step, the magic calls,
In shimmering whispers, evening falls.

Colors blend in a soft embrace,
Nature's tapestry finds its place.
The woodland waltzes, free and wild,
In the heart of every carefree child.

From the glade where the fae reside,
Flickers of joy cannot hide.
They twirl and spin in a graceful trance,
Weaving dreams in the woodland dance.

So gather 'round, dear friends of light,
Join the dance, take joyful flight.
In this circle where spirits prance,
Find your place in the woodland dance.

Sunlit Whispers Beneath the Canopy

Beneath the canopy's golden shade,
Sunlit whispers softly parade.
Secrets hidden in leaves so green,
Mysteries dance where none have been.

Gentle breezes carry the sound,
Of hidden realms all around.
Each note a story waiting to tell,
Of enchanted places, where spirits dwell.

Fern and flower in vibrant hues,
Celebrate every sunbeam's muse.
With each rustling, a tale begins,
Of laughter, of sorrow, and ancient sins.

In the stillness, hear the plea,
Of nature's heart that beats so free.
With eyes closed tight, let visions soar,
Through sunlit whispers forevermore.

Let the sunlight guide your feet,
Through the forest, serene and sweet.
In this embrace of emerald leaves,
Feel the magic that nature weaves.

Elven Echoes of Dappled Light

In the glen where the shadows sigh,
Elven echoes softly fly.
Dappled light through branches break,
Whispers of love in every wake.

Lingering notes of a distant song,
Where dreams and realities belong.
The forest holds its breath in grace,
As time slows down in this sacred space.

Glimmers dance on the forest floor,
Secrets of ages, tales of yore.
With every step, a tale unfolds,
Of brave adventures and hearts so bold.

Silhouettes in the evening glow,
Twisting pathways, come and go.
Each echo carries a heartfelt plea,
For magic found in simplicity.

So listen close when night descends,
To the elven songs, where magic blends.
In the twilight's soft, tender light,
Feel the warmth of elven might.

Light Weavers of the Sylvan Realm

In a grove where whispers play,
The light weavers dance and sway.
With every spark their fingers craft,
The night's allure, a gentle draft.

Moss beneath their nimble feet,
In twilight hush, their hearts do beat.
They spin the threads of dusk and dawn,
A tapestry of dreams reborn.

With silver beams and golden hue,
They bind the sky with colors new.
Each flicker sings of ancient lore,
Within the forest's secret door.

A gentle breeze, a melodic hum,
As starlit whispers start to come.
In sylvan realms where magic weaves,
The light weavers dance, and time believes.

Glint of Gold in Twilight's Arms

When twilight's arms embrace the night,
A glimmer gold, a wondrous sight.
Beneath the boughs where shadows grow,
The whispers of the past bestow.

A river flows with dreams untold,
Reflecting warmth, a glint of gold.
Each ripple weaves a story rare,
In twilight's grace, we feel the air.

The stars alight like gems above,
Cascading light, a dance of love.
The forest holds its breath in awe,
As nature spins her timeless law.

With every pulse, the dusk descends,
In twilight's hug, the silence bends.
Beneath the leaves, the secrets stay,
A glint of gold, then fades away.

Elven Echoes of Luminescent Dreams

In the forest's heart, where echoes dwell,
Elven whispers weave a spell.
Luminescent dreams take flight,
On silver beams that cut the night.

As soft as dew upon the ground,
Their voices rise without a sound.
Time loses grip, the past aligns,
Where ancient lore in starlight shines.

Through branches thick, past twilight's seam,
Their laughter lingers, like a dream.
Each note a thread, in moonlight spun,
A symphony as bright as sun.

The air dances with fragrant blooms,
As echoes pulse through woodsy rooms.
In every heart, a story stirs,
In elven light, a magic blurs.

Vibrant Threads in the Forest's Fabric

Among the leaves, where shadows play,
Vibrant threads weave night and day.
With nature's hand, they twist and turn,
In every hue, new worlds to learn.

Golden strands of morning's glow,
Intertwined with twilight's flow.
The paths are drawn with colors bold,
In forest's fabric, dreams unfold.

Each step we tread, a story spun,
In vibrant threads, we're almost one.
With whispers soft, the leaves confer,
In harmony, the woodland stirs.

Beneath the sky, the earth adorned,
With vibrant shades, we are reborn.
In every fiber, life abounds,
In forest's fabric, joy surrounds.

Ethereal Radiance in the Moonlit Glade

In the glade where shadows play,
Ethereal light begins its sway.
Whispers dance on gentle breeze,
As heart and soul find soothing ease.

Silver beams touch every leaf,
Creating beauty, beyond belief.
The nightingale begins to sing,
Her voice, a treasure, magic brings.

Stars above in velvet cloak,
We weave our dreams in words unspoke.
The moonlight paints a canvas bright,
A wonderland bathed in soft light.

Glimmers of hope in shadows cast,
Remind us of the moments past.
In twilight's grace, together we stand,
Playing our part in this enchanted land.

As night unfurls its velvet shroud,
We breathe in deep, both soft and loud.
Within this glade, where spirits roam,
We find our hearts, we find our home.

Glittering Dreams Among the Woodland Spirits

Among the trees, where whispers creep,
Glittering dreams weave thoughts so deep.
Woodland spirits dance and twirl,
In shimmering gowns, they gently swirl.

In every corner, magic flows,
Where moonlight glimmers, and twilight glows.
A secret world, so pure and bright,
Emerging softly from the night.

With silver mist, they paint the air,
Binding realms with tender care.
Every leaf, a story told,
Of dreams and wishes, bright and bold.

In this realm, where magic thrives,
Close your eyes and feel it rise.
Listen closely to the lore,
The woodland spirits hold much more.

Here in the twilight's gentle kiss,
Every heartbeat whispers bliss.
Embrace the dreams they softly share,
For in their presence, there's magic everywhere.

Golden Threads That Bind the Realm

Threads of gold weave through the air,
   Binding moments, light and rare.
   Each connection, strong and true,
     A tapestry of me and you.

Across the fields where daisies sway,
   Golden threads lead us on our way.
   Carved in time, our fates entwined,
     In every heartbeat, love aligned.

Through trials faced, together we stand,
   Weaving strength with a gentle hand.
   The threads of life in patterns flow,
     A guiding map to help us grow.

In laughter's echo, sorrow's sigh,
   Golden ties that never die.
   Forever linked, in joy and pain,
We find our way through sun and rain.

So hold each thread close to your heart,
   For from this weave, we'll never part.
   In every flicker, every glance,
The golden threads weave our romance.

Shimmering Secrets Beneath the Boughs

Beneath the boughs where shadows hide,
Shimmering secrets, side by side.
Every rustle tells a tale,
Of whispered dreams that never pale.

In twilight hours, the magic wakes,
As owls hoot and the stillness breaks.
Each secret murmured in the night,
Illuminates the forest's light.

Leaves shimmer softly, kissed by dew,
Guarding treasures, old and new.
Embrace the night; let wonders flow,
Through every path where dreams may grow.

A hidden world of starlit grace,
Awaits the heart's forgotten space.
With every glance, a truth unveiled,
In nature's embrace, we are hailed.

So linger here, let spirits roam,
These shimmering secrets lead us home.
In tales of yore, we shall believe,
Under the boughs, magic weaves.

Flickering Lumens in the Fey's Embrace

In shadows deep where fairies dance,
Flickering lights spin wild romance.
They whisper soft beneath the trees,
In night's cool grasp, a gentle breeze.

Their laughter floats on silvery air,
As moonbeams weave through darkened hair.
A tapestry of dreams unfolds,
Amongst the leaves, their magic molds.

With every glow, a secret shared,
In hidden realms where none have dared.
The earth beneath, alive with sound,
In fey's embrace, pure joy is found.

They beckon forth with softest call,
A world where stars and shadows fall.
Here every wish takes flight and gleams,
In flickering lumens, born of dreams.

So close your eyes and heed the night,
Let magic guide you with its light.
For in the fey's eternal play,
Lies the wonder of dreams' ballet.

Glowing Inflections of the Woodland Night

Beneath the canopy of whispering trees,
The night awakens with gentle ease.
Glowing inflections in shadows cast,
Every moment a spark, every breath a blast.

The chattering brook sings tunes so sweet,
Where woodland creatures come to greet.
Each flicker and shimmer, a tale retold,
In glades where secrets quietly unfold.

Fireflies blink in a rhythmic flow,
Lighting paths where soft winds blow.
They dance on air, a celestial flight,
In glowing inflections of the night.

Beneath the stars, enchantments twine,
As magic seeps through every line.
The heart of the forest beats with grace,
In every shadow, a warm embrace.

So wander forth, let wonder rise,
In the realm of the night, be wise.
For in each glow, a whisper flies,
A promise stitched in midnight skies.

Celestial Trails on the Elven Path

Through ancient woods where glories meet,
Celestial trails make the heart skip beat.
Elven footsteps soft as dew,
Lead us deeper, old yet new.

Stars align in their gentle play,
Guiding us on this mystical way.
With each step, the spirits sigh,
Beneath the arch of twilight sky.

The trees enchanted hold their breath,
Roots intertwined, defying death.
Glimmers twirl in harmony's weave,
In the silence, we dare to believe.

So follow the light where dreams reside,
With courage found, let hearts abide.
For on this path, we're truly free,
In elven grace, eternity.

Let whispers echo in the night,
As we traverse the path of light.
For every trail, a story spun,
On elven paths, we become one.

Lustrous Moments in the Misty Grove

In the misty grove, where magic swirls,
Each rustling leaf a secret unfurls.
Lustrous moments painted in dew,
Every heartbeat a promise anew.

The fog weaves dreams, soft as a sigh,
While starlit whispers beckon nigh.
In shadows play, the past takes flight,
Waltzing softly through velvet night.

With every step, the world transforms,
As nature's pulse in silence warms.
A fragrant breeze of earth and bloom,
In the grove's embrace, banish gloom.

The moonbeams twirl, a delicate grace,
As shimmering light fills every space.
Lost in wonder, we sway and glide,
In lustrous moments, love won't hide.

So carve your name in the misty air,
With whispers shared, a secret pair.
For in this grove, where time stands still,
Lustrous moments weave dreams at will.

Sparkling Lullabies in the Elderwood

Whispers of silver in twilight's embrace,
The stars gently dance, a delicate lace.
Dreams weave through branches, alive in their flight,
As the night glimmers softly, a quilt made of light.

A brook sings its secrets, a lullaby clear,
Crickets join in, their music sincere.
Each rustle and murmur, a tale to behold,
In the heart of the forest, where stories unfold.

Beneath moonlit arches, the shadows entwine,
The nightingale sings, with a voice so divine.
Sleep now, dear wanderer, lulled by the sound,
For magic is woven in dreams that abound.

Soft moss cushions softly, a bed for the weary,
While fireflies flicker, their glow never dreary.
Close your eyes gently, let the world slip away,
In Elderwood's arms, where you'll safely stay.

Morning will come, with the dawn's gentle sweep,
But for now, sleep sweetly, in nature's deep keep.
The sparkling lullabies will cradle your heart,
Until light breaks the silence, a brand new start.

Luminous Fragments in the Glade's Heart

In the glade's gentle heart, where shadows do play,
Luminous fragments dance, guiding the way.
Petals unfurl like secrets untold,
In a tapestry vibrant, of silver and gold.

Beneath towering willows, where silence abides,
Flickers of light weave through nature's wide strides.
Each sparkle a promise, each glimmer a sigh,
A whisper of magic that never will die.

Crystals of dew cling to the soft velvet grass,
Reflecting the wonders of time as they pass.
The air brims with stories from ages long past,
While the world holds its breath, in a moment so vast.

Listen close to the rustle, the chirp, and the call,
For luminous fragments are gifts for us all.
In the glade's tender bosom, enchantments unfold,
As secrets of nature dance bold and untold.

Hold on to the night, let it wrap you in dreams,
Where the glade's gentle heartbeat is more than it seems.
With each flickering light, let your worries take flight,
For in luminous fragments, everything feels right.

Dazzling Moments in the Fey Horizon

Golden rays spill forth from a sun-warmed sky,
Dazzling moments unfold as time flutters by.
In the fey horizon, where wonders ignite,
Every breath of the wind feels magically bright.

Petal-soft laughter echoes through glades,
Weaving through willows, hiding in shades.
Faeries play games, their joy pure and free,
While dancing on beams of sweet reverie.

The river of dreams flows with sapphire hues,
Where the breeze carries scents of wild blooms anew.
Every shimmer and spark, a story unbound,
In this realm of enchantment, true magic is found.

A tapestry woven with threads of delight,
Each dazzling moment a brief, blissful flight.
Hold close to the magic that life has to give,
For in the fey horizon, our spirits shall live.

Let not the shadows extinguish the flame,
In the dazzling dawn, life whispers your name.
Cherish each heartbeat, and let joy intertwine,
For in moments so precious, our souls truly shine.

Shining Whimsy of the Autumn Woods

In the autumn woods, the leaves paint the ground,
With colors that twirl, in a ballet unbound.
Shining whimsy dances on crisp, golden air,
Nature's own canvas, a masterful flare.

The whispers of breezes through branches do weave,
Stories of magic that none can believe.
Amidst laughter of squirrels, and the rustle of trees,
Time mingles with secrets, carried on leaves.

Underfoot, the crunching of memories past,
Each step a reminder of seasons that last.
In the dappled sunlight, where shadows skip play,
The whimsy of autumn turns night into day.

Flickers of ember beneath sky's deep embrace,
Remind us of warmth within nature's trace.
Gather round bonfires and let stories ignite,
As the autumn woods glisten with pure delight.

Hold tight to the magic that this season lends,
For whimsy and wonder are the bittersweet blends.
Beneath the bright harvest moon, love holds you near,
In the shining whimsy, let go of all fear.

Gilded Shadows in the Grove

In the grove where whispers dwell,
Gilded shadows weave their spell.
Leaves aflutter, secrets spun,
Underneath the waning sun.

Dancing lights in twilight's hue,
Promising dreams, both old and new.
Echoes glide through branches high,
Softly calling, as they sigh.

Moonlit paths that twist and turn,
Guide the hearts that long to learn.
Mysterious figures, cloaked in grace,
Beneath the oak's enchanted face.

In this realm of dusk and dawn,
Magic brews as fears are gone.
Gilded shadows, hand in hand,
With the dreams that life has planned.

Radiant Glints of the Mystical Circle

In the clearing, under stars,
Radiant glints and ancient scars.
Circle formed with whispered lore,
Gathered magic at the core.

Softly glowing, secrets call,
Every heartbeat, every fall.
Timeless echoes, visions bright,
Where the past meets future's light.

Crafted spells in moonbeams shown,
Underneath the trees that groan.
Chants arise from lips of grace,
Summoning a sacred space.

In this hallowed, quiet ground,
Mystic forces twist around.
Radiant glints of lost design,
In the silence, hearts align.

Embered Sparks in the Forest's Embrace

Embered sparks amongst the trees,
Flickering light on gentle breeze.
Hushed conversations, soft and low,
In the forest's warm glow.

Fantasy brews in every shade,
Ancient tales that never fade.
With each breath, a story weaves,
In the tapestry the night leaves.

Fireflies dance in joyful flight,
Illuminating the deepening night.
Every whisper stirs the air,
As the woodland's secrets share.

Ember's warmth in shadows cast,
Connecting future to the past.
In the quiet, we can see,
All the wonders meant to be.

Auras of Ancient Trees in Twilight

Auras glow in twilight's mist,
Ancient trees in soft embrace kissed.
Roots that seem to whisper tales,
Of forgotten, timeless trails.

Branches arching toward the sky,
Nurturing dreams that drift and fly.
In their shade, we come to rest,
Feeling every branch and crest.

Fables spin with every breeze,
Woven tightly through the leaves.
Echoes of a world once known,
In the ancient wood that's grown.

Touched by light of fading sun,
Tales of old begin to run.
Auras bright in twilight's calm,
Nature's song, a soothing balm.

Capricious Glimmers of the Fey Court

In shadows soft where whispers play,
The fey court twirls at end of day.
With laughter bright and eyes aglow,
They weave a dream, a mystic show.

Their capricious hearts like wild winds blow,
In secret glades, where few can go.
With petals fair and shimmering light,
They dance and spin till dawn's first sight.

A trickster's grin, a glance askew,
They beckon forth the brave and true.
With every step, the magic sings,
Among the trees, their joy takes wings.

Yet in their mirth, a warning lies,
To tread with care, for time quickly flies.
With fleeting glimpses, they depart,
Leaving echoes in the heart.

So cherish moments, swift like air,
In realms where time feels light as prayer.
For in the dance of fey delight,
We glimpse the magic of the night.

Golden Revelations Under Starry Canopies

Beneath the vast and shimmering skies,
The stars unveil their ancient guise.
With tales of old that softly gleam,
They whisper secrets, weave a dream.

Golden revelations wrapped in night,
The moon reflects their gentle light.
With every twinkle, hope ignites,
A dance of shadows, pure delights.

In cosmic paths where wishes soar,
The universe reveals its core.
Through silence deep, a message passed,
Eternal truths, from first to last.

The nightingale sings, a lonesome tune,
Echoing thoughts beneath the moon.
With every note, the stars align,
A symphony of fate divine.

So look above with yearning eyes,
In starlit dreams, your spirit flies.
For under these celestial beams,
Lie the seeds of countless dreams.

Twilit Gold of the Enchanted Realm

In twilit glades where shadows dwell,
The enchanted realm weaves a spell.
With golden hues that kiss the trees,
Each leaf a whisper in the breeze.

As twilight falls, the magic stirs,
With every breeze, the forest purrs.
Glittering trails where fairies roam,
This tranquil world feels just like home.

With every step, a tale unfolds,
Of love and loss, of hearts that hold.
The secrets linger in the air,
Embracing dreams, both near and rare.

Illumined paths of fleeting light,
The golden promise of the night.
In echoes lost, the owls call,
With wisdom deep, they guide us all.

So wander wide through dusk's embrace,
And find your place in nature's grace.
Among the twilit gold that gleams,
Breathe in the magic, live your dreams.

Ethereal Sparkles of the Woodland Dance

In wooded realms where fairies tread,
Ethereal sparkles softly spread.
With wings of gossamer, they soar,
In rhythm with the heart's own lore.

A dance of light on mossy floor,
They weave their spells, forevermore.
With laughter bubbling, they entwine,
In circles bright, their joy divine.

The night unfolds, a velvet cloak,
In every step, a story spoke.
As moonbeams play in twilight's grasp,
They celebrate in nature's clasp.

With silvered laughter, echoes ring,
The woodland's heart begins to sing.
In unity, each spirit prances,
With every beat, the magic dances.

So linger long in dusky shades,
And join the fey where beauty fades.
For in their sparkles, dreams are found,
In woodland dance, the world unbound.

Radiant Fables of the Elven Circle

In whispers soft, the legends weave,
Of timeless nights and tales believe.
With silver threads, the stories glow,
As ancient trees in silence grow.

Beneath the moon's enchanting light,
Elven hearts find pure delight.
With laughter sweet, they dance and sing,
While nature bows to welcome spring.

In every leaf, a secret stirs,
A magic known to only hers.
In twilight's gaze, their spirits soar,
And echo through the wooded lore.

Through glen and brook, the fables glide,
With every step, enchantments bide.
In tranquil glades where shadows drift,
The elven tales, a timeless gift.

The circle's heart, a sacred trust,
Bound by the earth, the air, the dust.
Their radiant fables intertwine,
In every secret, a story shines.

Flickering Gilt in the Glade's Secrets

Amidst the trees, a glimmer bright,
Gold sparkles dance in fading light.
The glade reveals its hidden charms,
With whispered secrets, nature warms.

In shimmering hues, the leaves do sway,
As twilight beckons the close of day.
Flickering fireflies take their flight,
A ballet spun from dreams of night.

Through shadows deep, where pathways bend,
The glade's allure will never end.
With gilded paths, adventure calls,
To where the ancient magic sprawls.

In every rustle, a tale unspooled,
Of whispered truths that fate has ruled.
The glade, a cradle of pure delight,
Guarding stories 'neath starry light.

With every breeze, the night unfolds,
The flickering glint of mysteries told.
In gentle realms where dreams reside,
The glade's secrets, an ethereal guide.

Shadows of Gold in the Hearth of Nature

In nature's hearth, shadows take flight,
With golden hues that kiss the night.
Among the brambles, secrets lay,
A song of life, both wild and fey.

The forest breathes, its essence flows,
As time stands still, the spirit grows.
With every glance, a tale of yore,
Where shadows waltz on the forest floor.

With whispers low, the tales arise,
Of ancient spirits, silvered skies.
In golden beams, the heart does gleam,
A tapestry spun from nature's dream.

The shadows dance, a fleeting thread,
With every step, a whisper spread.
In the hearth of nature's core,
Gold shadows linger, forevermore.

And in the quiet, the stories call,
Beneath the stars, we are all enthralled.
In nature's arms, we shall remain,
Embraced by shadows, the golden grain.

Shimmering Leaves Beneath Whirling Stars

Set free amidst the cosmic breeze,
Shimmering leaves with gentle ease.
Beneath the stars, a dance unfolds,
In silver whispers, magic holds.

As starlight spills on every bough,
Nature bows low, takes a vow.
In moonlit embrace, the earth awakes,
With every ripple, the silence shakes.

The leaves converse in twilight's glow,
Repeating tales of long ago.
Whirling stars weave dreams anew,
Through shimmering skies, a path to pursue.

In the hush of night, a lullaby sings,
Carried on air, the peace it brings.
With every twirl, the forest spins,
A dance of life where hope begins.

And as the dawn will softly rise,
The shimmering leaves reveal their guise.
Beneath the stars, our hearts align,
In nature's orchestra, we intertwine.

Sylvan Sparks Amidst the Fae

In forests deep where shadows play,
The fireflies dance at end of day.
With twinkling lights like stars set free,
They weave through dreams in harmony.

Beneath the boughs of ancient trees,
Whispers carried by the breeze.
The fae are laughing, soft and bright,
Their joy reflected in the night.

A glimmer here, a shimmer there,
A world alive, beyond compare.
With every flicker, tales unfold,
Of magic woven strong and bold.

In hidden glades, where secrets bloom,
The moonlight casts away the gloom.
So wanderers tread with gentle grace,
To find the fae in their embrace.

And when at last the dawn is near,
The sparkles fade but do not fear.
For in our hearts, the magic stays,
A sylvan spark that lights our ways.

Celestial Reflections on Gossamer Leaves

Beneath the canopies so wide,
Where sparkling gems of dew abide,
A mirror to the heavens shines,
In gossamer, the starlight aligns.

Each leaf a canvas, brushed with gold,
Stories whispered, secrets told.
The twilight sparkles on the ground,
In nature's art, our dreams are found.

The dance of shadows, soft and slow,
Reflects the moon's enchanted glow.
In quiet moments, time stands still,
As magic weaves its gentle thrill.

To wander lost in this pure night,
Where every breath ignites delight.
The fae will guide with tender air,
Through realms unseen, a blissful care.

In every leaf, a universe,
A world where we can all immerse.
So let us dream and let us believe,
In celestial tapestries we weave.

Luminous Orbs in the Fey's Domain

In twilight shades where night shall weave,
Luminous orbs of light believe.
They hover low, they shimmer bright,
Guiding travelers with their light.

Through winding paths and whispering glades,
The fae's soft laughter never fades.
With flicker here, and glow nearby,
Stars play hide and seek in the sky.

The gentle hum of magic sings,
As echoes dance on fairy wings.
With every step, the world transforms,
In fey's embrace, the heart conforms.

So come, dear friend, and take my hand,
To wander forth in this strange land.
Amongst the orbs of silver gleams,
We'll find the path where starlight dreams.

And when the dawn begins to break,
The orbs will fade, though hearts won't ache.
For in our souls they'll ever stay,
A light that guides us on our way.

Glimmering Pathways Through the Sylvan Realm

Through emerald aisles where spirits tread,
Glimmering pathways gently spread.
Each step a pulse of life anew,
In sylvan realms that sing for you.

With every rustle, secrets stir,
As faerie whispers start to blur.
Around us swirls a mystic dance,
Inviting all to take a chance.

The golden light, it threads the trees,
As if spun from the very breeze.
A world awaits with gates ajar,
The sweetest dreams, the brightest star.

In laughter shared and stories spun,
Together we can chase the sun.
Through glimmering paths where magic ties,
We'll find the truth beneath the skies.

So, mark this place within your heart,
For every end brings a new start.
In sylvan realms, where wonders lie,
The glimmers fade, yet never die.

Golden Gleams in the Enchanted Glade

In the glade where shadows play,
Golden beams of sunlight sway.
Softly whispers of dew-drenched leaves,
Nature's magic, the heart believes.

Crimson blooms in bright array,
Dancing freely with the day.
Butterflies, on gentle wing,
Flutter by, a fleeting spring.

Ancient trees with boughs so wide,
Guard the secrets they confide.
Echoes of the past resound,
In this haven, peace is found.

A brook runs clear, with laughter bright,
Its melody, pure delight.
Frogs and crickets join the song,
In the glade, where dreams belong.

As twilight falls, the fireflies gleam,
A dance of stars, a silver dream.
Magic lingers in the skies,
In the glade, where the heart flies.

Whispering Winds of the Fey Realm

Winds that whisper through the trees,
Carry scents of nectar's tease.
In the fey realm, dreams entwine,
Where the shadows softly shine.

Leaves that rustle, soft and low,
Songs of secrets, ever flow.
Dancing lights like spirits play,
In the heart of night and day.

Gliding fairies, laughter sweet,
Tiptoe on the night's soft sheet.
Wings aflutter, like the breeze,
Stirring tales of ancient seas.

Stars above in glistening rows,
Guide the fey through twilight's throes.
Every heartbeat sings a tune,
In the glow of the silver moon.

Time stands still in this mystic land,
Nature's palette, hand in hand.
Whispering winds, forever near,
In the fey realm, no need for fear.

Luminous Threads in the Elven Dance

Threads of starlight weave and spin,
In elven hearts, where dreams begin.
With nimble feet on dew-kissed grass,
They twirl and glide, the moments pass.

Moonlit laughter fills the air,
Each step taken with utmost care.
Spirits twine in joy's embrace,
A waltz that time cannot erase.

Glimmering gowns that shimmer bright,
Reflect the magic of the night.
Elven eyes, like emerald fire,
Dance with passion, never tire.

Flute notes rise, a symphony,
Each note a part of memory.
In this realm, where time does flow,
Every heartbeat, softly aglow.

As dawn approaches, fears take flight,
A final spin in morning light.
Threads of joy cling to the morn,
In the dance where dreams are born.

Gilded Echoes Beneath Moonlit Canopies

Beneath the moon's soft, gilded glow,
Echoes stir from long ago.
Leaves entwined in silver light,
Whisper tales that grace the night.

Glimmers dance on dew-drenched grass,
Moments lost, yet none can pass.
Time suspends in quiet air,
Enchanted whispers lead to dare.

Branches weave a canopy,
Guarding secrets, wild and free.
Owls call softly, nightbirds sing,
In this place, where magic clings.

Flickering lights, as stars take flight,
Guide the wanderer through the night.
Each step forward, a heartbeat shared,
In the woods, where souls are bared.

As dawn breaks through the jeweled trees,
Echoes fade upon the breeze.
Yet in dreams, they linger still,
Beneath the moon, we seek to fill.

Glinting Whispers of Evergreen Spirits

In the heart of the wood, secrets sigh,
Where tall trees nod with a knowing eye.
Moss carpets ground like a verdant cloak,
While stars in the branches, softly folk.

Beneath the moon's watch, shadows dance,
Glow of the fairies, a fleeting chance.
Whispers of spirits, old tales unfold,
In emerald depths, stories retold.

Each breeze carries laughter, each crackle, a song,
Where nature's own magic has dwelt all along.
Amongst the wild ferns, new dreams intertwine,
Glinting with joy, like sunlight's pure shine.

Glimmers at dusk light the forest's grand hall,
As creatures emerge to heed the night's call.
With rustling leaves, the enchantment grows bright,
In the glinting whispers, we lose track of night.

Swaying with rhythm, as twilight descends,
Life resonates softly, as daylight rescinds.
In endless embrace, the spirits take flight,
Guiding the wanderers through the silver moonlight.

Ethereal Gold in the Twilight Meadow

In twilight's embrace, where shadows are spun,
Glimmers of gold spark, as day comes undone.
The meadows, they shimmer, with secrets untold,
In whispers of dusk, as the colors unfold.

Beneath starry veils, the flowers awake,
Soft petals unfold with each gentle shake.
A wind carries tales from a past long ago,
In a language of light, where dreams freely flow.

The fireflies flicker in unison fair,
Dancing in patterns, a magical air.
With every soft rustle, new stories arise,
Beneath the crafting of twilight's kind skies.

Nature's grand canvas, painted in hues,
The pulse of the earth sings secretive clues.
Breathe in the magic, let worries all fade,
In the glittering meadow, peace is remade.

As darkness deepens, the stars take their place,
Casting soft shadows, enchanting the space.
In ethereal whispers, the night softly calls,
While the heartbeat of magic within us enthralls.

Twinkling Visions of the Elven Veil

Beyond the thick veil where the twilight weeps,
Twinkling visions awaken from dreams and deep sleeps.
In realms draped in silver, enchantment we find,
Where whispers of elves, in the distance unwind.

Light dances on water with shimmering grace,
As moonlight conjures shadows that play and embrace.
In each glinting drop, ethereal gleam,
Beckoning all to follow the dream.

Here, butterflies flit in a waltz so divine,
Each flutter a note in a rare, sacred line.
Nectar and twilight in a choiring song,
To the rhythm of hours that linger so long.

Through thickets of silver, a pathway unfolds,
Leading to wonders and tales yet untold.
With each step we take, the night seems to glow,
In twinkling visions, hidden seeds we sow.

Castles of starlight in elven domain,
Where laughter and music intertwine with the rain.
In the breath of the night, magic flows like a stream,
And within the elven veil, we become what we dream.

Sunbeam Patterns in the Forest Court

In the forest court where the sunbeams play,
Patterns of light weave stories each day.
Leaves shimmer gently, like whispers of gold,
While secrets of nature in stillness unfold.

As branches embrace the warm sun's bright rays,
A mosaic of shadows in intricate maze.
Every flicker of light, a breath of delight,
Guiding lost wanderers through passages bright.

Beams dance like faeries on skirts of the trail,
Filling the air with a sweet, calming veil.
The heart of the forest pulsates and churns,
In the flickering glow, wisdom returns.

Gentle and tender, the breezes entwine,
Soft whispers of stories in every design.
With each glowing moment, the earth softly sways,
In the warmth of the sun, in the dance of the rays.

In laughter of streams and the rustle of leaves,
The court is alive, and the heart truly believes.
While sunlight embraces each creature and stone,
In the patterns of life, we're never alone.

Glowing Circles of Legacies Untold

In shadows deep where secrets hide,
Whispers of past in silence glide.
Legacy twinkles in the night,
A soft glow, a fading light.

Each circle holds a tale of yore,
Fragments of dreams that once did soar.
With every step, a story spun,
Of battles lost and victories won.

Remembered names in twilight's embrace,
Ghostly echoes in time's vast space.
Glowing paths that lead us home,
Through haunted woods where legends roam.

The ancient trees stand tall and wise,
Guardians of truths beneath the skies.
With roots that twist in tangled grace,
They harbor lives in every place.

So gather round these fires bright,
Let tales revive in the gentle night.
For in each heart, a story sleeps,
In glowing circles, memory keeps.

Flickering Lights Beneath the Starry Canopy

Beneath a blanket of velvet skies,
Flickers of dreams like stars arise.
With every spark, a wish takes flight,
In the heart of the deep, silent night.

Whispers of breezes dance with glee,
Painting the world in mystery.
Each light a beacon, a guiding flare,
Leading lost souls through twilight air.

The moon, a guardian of secrets shared,
Holds the hopes of wanderers who dared.
In this vast expanse, hearts intertwine,
United in wonder, their spirits align.

Luminous whispers weave through the dark,
A tapestry of dreams where souls embark.
With every flicker and glimmer of light,
They dance with shadows, taking flight.

So let us gather close, hand in hand,
Beneath this celestial, shimmering band.
For in the night, our dreams take form,
As flickering lights keep our hearts warm.

Whirling Wonders in the Enchanted Field

In the meadow where wildflowers sway,
Magic dances, come what may.
Whirling wonders beneath the sun,
A tapestry of life has begun.

The breeze sings sweet with every turn,
Nature's grace, in hearts, it burns.
Each fluttering leaf, a tale it tells,
In the enchanted field where laughter dwells.

With the sun dipping low, the colors blaze,
Golden hues set the sky ablaze.
A symphony played by the wind's caress,
In this realm of wonder, we feel blessed.

As dusk arrives and shadows creep,
The field awakens from its sleep.
A shift in magic, the night unfurls,
A waltz of dreams in the moonlight swirls.

So let us dance where magic weaves,
In the enchanted field, where spirit believes.
With every step, let joy resound,
In whirling wonders, our hearts are found.

Charm of the Brightwood Realm

In the heart of the Brightwood, secrets lie,
Where sunlight filters through branches high.
A realm of wonder, so rich and bright,
Whispers of magic in the soft daylight.

Golden leaves flutter in the gentle breeze,
Each one a treasure, a moment to seize.
Soft laughter echoes through the glade,
In this enchanted space, memories are made.

With each step deeper, the wonder expands,
In this enchanting land where nature stands.
Charmed by the beauty, heart open wide,
Finding solace in where dreams abide.

The flowers bloom with vibrant hues,
In this realm, we're free to choose.
To weave our sorrows and joys anew,
In the charm of the Brightwood, forever true.

So gather near the ancient trees,
Feel the pulse of life in the gentle breeze.
For in this realm, dreams dare to meet,
With the charm of the Brightwood, life is sweet.

Glistening Paths in the Heart of the Forest

In the woods where shadows play,
Glistening paths weave night and day.
Whispers of leaves in gentle sway,
Secrets linger, lost in the fray.

Moonlight drapes the ancient trees,
A symphony of night-time breeze.
Footsteps soften on the moss,
Nature's treasure, a hidden gloss.

Twinkling stars peek through the boughs,
The forest's magic gently rouses.
Every turn a tale to spin,
Where journeys start, where dreams begin.

Footprints etched in silvery dew,
Stories shared by a wise old rue.
The roots entangle deep with care,
Whispering hopes in the cool night air.

In glimmers bright the forest beams,
Filling hearts with silken dreams.
Adventure calls with every glance,
In the woods, we lose ourselves in chance.

Whispered Flames of Faery Light

In twilight's grasp, where secrets glow,
Whispered flames begin to flow.
Faery lights in a dance so bold,
Tales of wonder, softly told.

Glimmers flicker, shadows weave,
In magic's heart, do we believe?
Each spark a wish, a dream's delight,
Casting hope in the soft night.

With every breath, the world feels near,
Voices echo, sweet and clear.
Elders nod in the softest tone,
Guiding each heart, never alone.

A flick of dust, a flurry of light,
Carried along by the wings of night.
In the air, a laughter entwined,
Glimmers of joy we seek and find.

Through the embers, a path ignites,
Guided by whispered faery rites.
Hand in hand, we shall embark,
Together, we'll bloom from the dark.

Luminary Threads in the Enchanted Ether

In the ether, threads do gleam,
Woven with care, like a dream.
Each luminary a guiding star,
Pulling our hearts from near and far.

Entwined in fate, the patterns show,
Whispers of light in a graceful flow.
Mystical echoes fill the air,
With every breath, a hidden prayer.

Journey forth on paths unknown,
Find the seeds of love we've sown.
Bathed in starlight's velvet hue,
Every moment feels so true.

Threads of fate, both dark and bright,
Dance around in the soft twilight.
Wrapped in warmth, our spirits soar,
In the ether, forevermore.

With every heartbeat, magic grows,
In the unseen, a river flows.
In tangled webs, our dreams take flight,
Guided by luminary light.

Glimmering Spirits of the Celestial Dance

Under skies where stardust twirls,
Glimmering spirits weave and whirl.
In cosmic tides, they take their flight,
Emboldened by the cloak of night.

With every step, the heavens sway,
Celestial dancers in grand array.
The moon, a witness to their grace,
In the night's embrace, they find their place.

Echoes of laughter, a joyous sound,
In the universe, their hearts abound.
Every swirl spins the threads of fate,
Spirits igniting destinies innate.

Through swirling mists, they weave their art,
Painting dreams upon the heart.
A melody of the night's romance,
In every movement, a soulful chance.

As dawn approaches, they shall flee,
Leaving behind a memory.
Yet in our hearts, their light will stay,
Glimmering spirits, forever at play.

Radiant Hues in Mythical Circles

In the glen where shadows dance,
Colors twinkle, bright romance.
Winds whisper secrets soft and sweet,
As ancient tales and spirits meet.

Emerald leaves in sunlight weave,
A tapestry that won't deceive.
Golden light spills from above,
Embracing all with endless love.

Glimmers of magic in the air,
Every moment a precious flare.
Through arches of the silver trees,
A melody rides the gentle breeze.

Beneath the stars, enchanted ground,
Lost souls awaken, hope unbound.
In this realm where dreams reside,
The heart feels free, no need to hide.

With every shade, a story told,
Of valiant knights and hearts of gold.
So join the dance and take your place,
In radiant hues, find your grace.

Shimmering Flashes of the Sylvan Night

Underneath the velvet skies,
Where the forest softly sighs,
Stars flicker like a candle's glow,
Whispers of magic dance below.

Moonbeams trace a pathway bright,
Leading wanderers through the night.
With every step, a secret friend,
In the shadows, they gently blend.

Moths weave tales in silver light,
Fluttering wings in joyous flight.
Crickets sing their soothing song,
A symphony where dreams belong.

By ancient oaks, the faeries play,
In shimmering glades where fairies sway.
With joyful hearts, they twirl and spin,
Enchanted nights are where we begin.

Magic glows in every sigh,
An echo of the earth and sky.
In the sylvan night's embrace,
Find your magic, find your place.

Aurous Fragments in the Woodland Dream

In the hush of the morning light,
A golden shimmer, pure delight.
Dewdrops gather on blades of grass,
Each glint a moment meant to pass.

Through tangled roots and whispering leaves,
The woodland breathes, the heart believes.
A chorus sweet of nature's grace,
In every nook, time leaves a trace.

A trail of gold leads us along,
Where every sound is a gentle song.
From tranquil brooks, the laughter flows,
Carving paths where the wild rose grows.

Fragments of sunbeams brightly play,
Guiding hearts that have lost their way.
In dreams, we wander, vast and free,
Discovering what we long to be.

In the woodland's warm embrace,
Adventures stir in time and space.
Aurous moments, bright and bold,
Gathered dreams, forever hold.

Celestial Spirals in the Faerie Grove

In the grove where magic gleams,
Celestial spirals weave our dreams.
Stars twirl down like twinkling fire,
Igniting hearts with wild desire.

With every step on mossy ground,
Hidden wonders, pure joy abound.
Whispers of ancients call us near,
In the silence, the truth is clear.

Cradled by the ivy's embrace,
Time meanders in this sacred space.
Here, hopes take flight, fears release,
In the dance of the night, find peace.

Crystal petals in moonlit dew,
Bathe the world in a wondrous hue.
Faerie laughter fills the air,
Every moment, a spark to share.

So join the dance, let spirits soar,
In celestial spirals forevermore.
In the faerie grove, where bright hearts meet,
Feel the magic beneath your feet.

Threads of Light in the Sylvan Tapestry

In glades where shadows softly weave,
The golden threads of light conceive,
They dance upon the leaves so bright,
A tapestry of day and night.

Each whisper of the breeze that flows,
Brings secrets where the magic grows,
With every spark and gentle gleam,
The forest sings a tender dream.

With roots entwined in ancient lore,
The trees hold tales of yore in store,
Their knotted branches stretch and swell,
In this enchanted sylvan dell.

The wildflowers nod in bold delight,
As colors burst to greet the light,
In every hue, a story blooms,
Within this realm where beauty looms.

So wander through the dappled shade,
And let your heart be unafraid,
For in the woods, where magic's spun,
You'll find the paths where dreams are done.

Whispers of Gilded Dawn in the Faerie Grove

As dawn spills gold through leafy seams,
Soft whispers weave through waking dreams,
The faerie folk in gossamer play,
Dance lightly in the break of day.

With laughter ringing, crystal clear,
The dew-kissed blooms draw ever near,
Each petal blushes, soaked in sun,
While nature sings, the day's begun.

Misty veils of twilight fade,
As shadows lengthen in the glade,
Secrets shared on morning's breath,
A timeless spell of life and death.

Beneath the boughs of ancient trees,
The rustling leaves sway with the breeze,
In every gust, there's magic spun,
The faerie grove awakes, then runs.

A gilded dawn of mystic hues,
Where every heart finds joy to choose,
So step beneath this verdant dome,
And let the grove feel like your home.

Golden Winks in the Woodland Whisper

In twilight's blush where shadows sigh,
The woodland whispers low and shy,
With golden winks that flicker bright,
Each beam of sun a fleeting light.

Among the bramble, soft and sweet,
The forest hums a gentle beat,
Time lingers here in nature's care,
Where dreams float lightly in the air.

With trails unknown, the branches bend,
Each step a dance, as fairies send,
Their laughter laced with summer's cheer,
A melody for all to hear.

The ferns unfurl, the daisies sway,
While twilight kisses end of day,
A secret kept by woods entwined,
For those who seek, the heart will find.

So cherish all the quiet sights,
And listen for those golden lights,
For in this realm of whispered tune,
Magic ignites beneath the moon.

Elven Sunbeams Dancing on Mossy Stones

In glimmering glades where dreams take flight,
Elven sunbeams paint the night,
They twirl and spin on mossy stones,
In this world where the wild wind moans.

With whispers soft as twilight's sigh,
The ancient trees stretch to the sky,
Their roots in secrets, deep and vast,
In silent homage to the past.

The shimmering light through branches creep,
Awakens echoes from their sleep,
Each beam a thread of golden grace,
That weaves through time, a warm embrace.

Among the ferns, the shadows play,
As dusk descends and steals the day,
Yet in this realm, the spirits gleam,
Like stars awakened from a dream.

So linger long where magic flows,
Among the stones where wonder grows,
For in this light, both bright and warm,
Elven whispers keep the heart from harm.

Sun-Kissed Threads in the Elven Glow

In the forest where shadows weave,
Sun-kissed threads the daylight cleave.
Elven whispers fill the air,
Dancing light beyond compare.

Mossy paths that twinkle bright,
Guide us through the dappled light.
Glimmers of a ancient tale,
On the breeze, the spirits sail.

Velvet petals, colors bold,
Woven tales in sunlight told.
Through the leaves, the sun does fall,
Casting magic, binding all.

A twirl of laughter, soft and sweet,
Elven hearts with joy entreat.
Songs of old, forever sung,
In the glow, we are all young.

Where shadows spill in emerald hues,
Nature's canvas, rich with views.
In the stillness, dreams take flight,
In the Elven glow, pure delight.

Radiance of the Dancing Elves

Underneath the silver moon,
Dancing elves in glimmering tune.
Wings of starlight all around,
Joyful laughter fills the ground.

Circling round the ancient oak,
Whispers of the forest spoke.
Their radiant forms bright and bold,
In the night, like tales of old.

Every twirl, a spark ignites,
In the dark, enchanting lights.
Magic swirls in every beat,
Underneath their dancing feet.

With every step, the shadows fade,
In their wake, a light parade.
Dreamers lost in moonlit grace,
Find their heartbeats in this place.

The night wraps close, a tender shroud,
In the forest, lost and found.
Radiance that never ends,
In the dance, the child descends.

Beam and Bloom in the Faery Light

In the glen where faeries play,
Blooming flowers greet the day.
Sunbeams filter through the boughs,
Painting magic on their brows.

With laughter sweet, they intertwine,
In every petal, stardust shine.
The air is thick with fragrant bliss,
In every breath, a faery kiss.

Softly glows the twilight hue,
As the stars arise anew.
With every bloom, a wish takes flight,
In the whispers of the night.

Emerging sprites with tiny wings,
Dance upon the forest springs.
With every beam, they weave and spin,
A tapestry where dreams begin.

Beneath the arch of silver beams,
In their light, the forest gleams.
Together, hearts both brave and true,
In faery light, we find our view.

Mystical Glimmers and Elfin Lore

In the mist of ancient woods,
Mystical glimmers, nature's goods.
Elfin lore dances in the breeze,
Tales of wonder amongst the trees.

Whispers weave through every leaf,
Stories hold the heart's belief.
In every shadow, secrets hide,
Inviting souls to step inside.

Cascading streams like silver threads,
Guide us where the forest spreads.
Each ripple holds a memory,
A glimpse of timeless reverie.

In moonlit glades where creatures roam,
Elves and dreams find their home.
Casting spells with every glance,
In the night, we join the dance.

So listen close to twilight's song,
In the magic where we belong.
Glimmers spark the heart's delight,
In elfin lore, we take to flight.

Glimmers of Magic in Mystic Rings

In the heart of the forest, secrets lie,
Whispers of ancients beneath the sky.
Glimmers of magic in rings of light,
Dance with the shadows, taking flight.

Waves of enchantment weave through the trees,
Softly they call on the wandering breeze.
Charmed by the echoes of time's gentle song,
The night holds its breath where dreams belong.

Stars twinkle shyly through drapes of dark,
Each twinkling spark a journey to embark.
In the stillness where moonbeams play,
A tapestry of wonders beckons the way.

Mystic rings call to those who believe,
Stories unfurl, and hearts will conceive.
A world wrapped in magic, threads intertwining,
Lending the lost and lonely their shining.

So gather, dear heart, to the twilight's embrace,
Where glimmers of magic find sacred space.
With each step you take, with each breath anew,
The world shares its secrets, a gift just for you.

Dappled Light Through Canopied Dreams

Beneath the green where the canopy sways,
Dappled light dances in delicate rays.
Whispers of hope ride the breath of the leaves,
Entwining the heart, weaving tales like weaves.

Moonlit paths beckon the wandering soul,
A tapestry woven where visions console.
Soft echoes of laughter between shaded glades,
Where time is a breeze, and the magic cascades.

Dreams float like petals on warm summer air,
Carrying wishes to those who dare.
In glimmers of sunlight, shadows embrace,
A haven for secrets, a mystical place.

With eyes wide as starlight, we wander this land,
Grasping for moments too fleeting to stand.
Each journey unveils a new part of the scene,
Dappled light over our canopied dreams.

So let your heart wander where sunlight abounds,
In dappled dreams, where the magic surrounds.
With stars as your guide, and wonder your seam,
Lose yourself gently in this radiant dream.

Flickering Shadows of Elvish Lore

In glades where the ancient elixirs brew,
Flickering shadows tell stories anew.
Whispers of elves weave through twilight's shroud,
Lending their wisdom, both gentle and proud.

The trees stand as sentinels guarding the night,
Holding the secrets of purest delight.
In echoes of laughter, the past finds its form,
As shadows embrace of the evening warm.

Elvish songs linger like silk in the air,
Carried through twilight with delicate care.
Each flicker of flame paints the tale of your heart,
Binding enchanted worlds, never to part.

With every soft breeze, a promise takes flight,
Flickering shadows reveal realms of light.
Amongst the glimmers, a journey unfolds,
As dusk weaves its magic in stories untold.

So heed the call where the shadows entwine,
In the cadence of night, your spirit will shine.
With flickering joys lighting all that's obscure,
Embrace the elvish, mysterious and pure.

Bright Inflections in the Dusk's Embrace

In the twilight's glow, where day meets the night,
Bright inflections shimmer, a marvelous sight.
Colors of dreams swirl in spectrums so bold,
Whispering tales of the dusk to be told.

Crickets begin their serenade to the stars,
While fireflies mimic the light of afar.
Each flicker a moment, a heartbeat of grace,
As dusk weaves its magic in time's soft embrace.

The horizon stretches, painting skies anew,
With strokes of enchantment in hues made for you.
Beneath the deep canopy, night softly hums,
While bright inflections of wonder it drums.

Stories unfold in the dusky parade,
As wishes unfurl in the twilight's cascade.
Whispers of old paint the world in delight,
In bright inflections, where shadows ignite.

So gather your dreams as the stars softly dance,
In the tenderness of dusk, take your chance.
With bright inflections, embrace the unknown,
For magic lies hidden where the heart has grown.

Fabled Flickers Beneath the Willow's Heart

Beneath the willow, whispers sweet,
A tapestry of shadows meet.
The flickers dance, a secret art,
Each spark a tale, an ancient part.

The night air hums with tales untold,
Of magic deep, both brave and bold.
With every glint, a memory spins,
Of laughter shared, where love begins.

In twilight's embrace, dreams intertwine,
With every flicker, a story divine.
The willow sways, a gentle guide,
As fabled echoes within confide.

Crickets serenade, a soft refrain,
While moonlit beams break through the rain.
In this sacred grove, magic flows,
Where time suspends, and wonder grows.

So linger here, where shadows play,
And let your heart find its way.
For amidst the flickers, you'll discover,
The magic within, forever to hover.

Mysterious Glimmers in Faery Paths

In the glade where faeries dwell,
Soft glimmers weave a wondrous spell.
A realm unseen by human eyes,
Where laughter dances, and magic flies.

Footsteps light on emerald moss,
In secret corners, paths across.
Each shimmer speaks of dreams untold,
Of mysteries wrap in silver and gold.

A flicker here, a twinkle there,
Fleeting forms in the scented air.
With every spark, a wish does soar,
Calling forth the tales of yore.

Beneath the arch of swirling trees,
The gentle sigh of whispering breeze.
Each glimmer tells of joys and fears,
Of hopes that shimmer through the years.

As night unfolds, a waltz begins,
With moonlit echoes, a dance of sins.
In faery paths, together we glide,
Embraced by magic, side by side.

Radiance of the Moonlit Fens

In moonlit fens where shadows play,
A radiant glow starts to sway.
The water glimmers in soft embrace,
Reflecting dreams in a silvery space.

Cattails whisper to the night,
While stars above blink with delight.
A chorus of frogs sings in tune,
Their voices echo beneath the moon.

Each ripple tells a story rare,
Of wanderers lost in crystal air.
The moon, a guardian watching o'er,
Bringing peace to the fens' soft shore.

In this embrace of twilight's breath,
Life dances close to the edge of death.
Yet here in shadows, hearts align,
In moonlit fens, love's light will shine.

So let your soul be led with grace,
To where the world holds its gentle space.
For in the night, beneath the sky,
The radiance shines, as spirits fly.

Enchanted Fireflies in the Woodland Dance

In the woodland deep where secrets sigh,
Fireflies twinkle like stars on high.
An enchanted dance in the cool night air,
Where magic lingers, free from care.

They swirl like thoughts in a dreamy trance,
Each spark ignited in a playful glance.
Around the trees, they weave their light,
Guiding the lost through endless night.

A symphony of whispers fills the space,
As fireflies paint the darkness with grace.
Soft glows enchant the heart so true,
With promises made in the evening dew.

As shadows waltz with the glowing beams,
Lost in the folds of impossible dreams.
The woodland alive, a spirit's chance,
In the tender embrace of this firefly dance.

So take a breath, let go of haste,
And join the revelry, a moment to taste.
In the heart of the night, find your romance,
With enchanted fireflies, lost in their dance.

www.ingramcontent.com/pod-product-compliance
Ingram Content Group UK Ltd.
Pitfield, Milton Keynes, MK11 3LW, UK
UKHW021439280125
4335UKWH00035B/316